A

A Mountain Alphabet

B

TEXT BY MARGRIET RUURS
ART BY ANDREW KISS

TUNDRA BOOKS

C

A MOUNTAIN ALPHABET

Mountains are an impressive sight anywhere in the world. But our mountains in North America offer a variety of riches that is unique. The ranges are home to emerald lakes beneath snowcapped peaks, tall pines and magnificent maples, birds that swoop down to rivers teeming with fish. Mountains and foothills hold secrets and surprises that fill you with excitement as you come across an animal in its natural surroundings or watch a bald eagle soaring on an updraft.

It has taken hundreds of millions of years for our mountains to get the shapes they have today. Some mountains have their roots as volcanoes; others started out as swampy deltas and ocean bottoms. Those closest to the Pacific Ocean are uplifted igneous rock. Our Rocky Mountains are layers of mud-like (sedimentary) rock thrust up, folded and bent by the incredible forces of nature. The biggest change came during the ice age when the northern part of the continent was covered by glacial ice.

Though they look massive and solid, mountains are still constantly changing. A drop of water, a crystal of ice, a puff of wind are the tools that sculpt rock into ever-changing shapes.

Even if you have never seen a mountain, did you know that they affect the way you live? Mountains are the gathering places for snow and rain and the starting point for the rivers that bring you water. Mountains affect air masses blowing across the sky and can cause rain, snow or drought. Mountains even dictate which way a river flows! The Continental Divide causes water to flow either east to the Atlantic Ocean, north to the Arctic Ocean, west to the Pacific Ocean, or south to the Gulf of Mexico.

Mountains hold many treasures such as real gold nuggets, silver and gems. But also treasures like delicate orchids, grizzly bears, and some of the last wilderness on earth. Walking along a trail, you may glimpse deer browsing on leaves, hear the hollow hammering of a woodpecker, or notice the musky smell of a mushroom.

Mountain climbers feel the mysterious force that compels them to risk their lives climbing the highest peaks simply "because they are there"!

Mountains divide but they also protect; they isolate but they also invite. You can study mountains for a lifetime, learn the names of every flower and rock. But nothing matches the experience of standing on the shore of a crystal blue lake and looking up at ragged ridges topped with icing-sugar snow. When you feel the day's first rays of sunlight on your shoulder and the wind blowing off the icefields in your face, you are simply filled with awe and wonder.

No matter how much time you spend in the mountains – a few days or the rest of your life – few things will touch your heart as powerfully as the wildness of mountains!

So come, put on your hiking boots and take a walk with us through the majestic mountains of western North America. Artist Andrew Kiss and I hope that this book will help you experience the thrill of the mountains that we live among and love.

To encourage you to look closely at both the mountains and each illustration, Andrew has hidden the relevant letter of the alphabet in each oil painting. For instance, you'll find the letter A in the first painting in the rocks of the upper right-hand corner.

Have fun!

Margriet.

A   Avalanche slopes are aglow with aspen in autumn.   a

B   A black bear browses on berries in the boreal forest.   **b**

Climbers cling to the canyon wall. C

D Deer detect danger among daisies and dandelions. d

E   Elks' bugling echoes through the evergreens.   e

F   A fisherman fly-fishes not far from fast flowing falls.   f

G   A gigantic grizzly digs for grubs in the grassy meadow.   g

H   We hike hairpin trails to higher and higher peaks.   h

I   I fly down the icy incline as if I had wings.   i

J Jason joins Jesse for a jog among the junipers. j

K From our kayak we see Kokanee salmon spawning. k

L   A loon's laughter lingers across the lake.   l

M Massive mountains loom in early morning mist. m

N   At night the naturalist tells about nocturnal animals.   n

O Overlooking the river, I observe an oblivious otter. O

P   We picnic by a parking lot in the provincial park.   p

 Q   Quit quarrelling with quilled creatures, Quincy!   q

R Rambunctious raccoons can be real rascals! r

Spawning salmon slowly swim up the shallow creek.

T   The train takes tourists through tunnels.   t

U

No U-turns on an upgrade!

u

V The victim ventured too far on the vertical slope. V

I went for a walk in a winter wonderland.

| X | X signs help wildlife and x-country skiers cross safely. | X |

Y   Yearlings lie among yarrow and yellow goldenrod.   **y**

Z   Mountain goats zip up the zigzagging trail.   Z

How many things did you find in each illustration? Did you find the hidden letter in each painting? Here is a list of what we know is out there, waiting to be discovered:

Aa alpine, avalanche slope, antlers, aspen, alder, animal, ant (on the antler); flowers: asters

Bb blueberries, boulders, branches, bark, black bear, butterfly, blue backpack, bighorn, bushes, beaver tree, bunny, boughs; bird: mountain bluebird

Cc climbers, cougar, cascading creek, chipmunk, canyon, cave, crystal clear water, conifers, cedars; birds: crow, chickadees; flowers: columbine

Dd deer (they are does), dragonfly, deciduous forest, dogwood, dead fall, decomposing material, design (in the spider web), digging bear; birds: dabbling ducks; flowers: dandelions, daisies

Ee elk, evergreens, erosion, ermine, ears (on the hare); bird: eagle

Ff fisherman, four fish, frog, forest, fir, feathers, fire lookout, falls, fly-fishing rod, foothills, Ford, fox; bird: falcon; flowers: fireweed, foxgloves

Gg glacier, grasses, granite, grizzly bear, groundhog, ground squirrel; birds: geese, gray jay, grouse, great gray owl; flowers: gentians, goldenrod, geranium, gumweed

Hh hikers, headwall, hiking boots, hummingbird (on the pack's emblem), herd of horned sheep, hat, helicopter, hiking trail map, hairpin trail, hoary marmot; bird: hawk. The entire picture represents the animals' habitat.

Ii icicles, incline, island of trees, icy surface

Jj junipers, joggers, jogging suits, jagged peaks and rocks; birds: juncos, jays (Stellar's Jay); Jason is wearing jewelry.

Kk kayak, Kokanee salmon, knapsack; bird: kingfisher

Ll Lake Louise, London and lynx (on t-shirts), lightning; birds: loons; flowers: lupines, lilies

Mm moose, mule deer, moss, mountains, mushrooms, marsh, muskrat, monarch butterfly; birds: magpie, merganser, mallard; flowers: marsh marigold, monkhood, milkweed. The geese are migrating. The deer and moose are mammals. And the whole picture has a mirror image!

Nn nine people, needle trees, night hawk (in the book), number 9 on sweater, newspaper, novel, necklace

Oo otter, outcrop of rock, orange; birds: oriole, owl, osprey

Pp peak, picnic tables, people, parking lot, pull-off, pickup truck, puddle, pond, Porsche, photographer, pica, provincial park sign, path, playing, no parking sign, privy (outhouse), pines, poplar, pumpkin pie, plate full of plums and peaches, puppy; plants: pinks, phlox

Qq quills, quilt with question marks and "Q" design, quartz, pie with one-quarter missing, book *Quest* by K.C. Queen; flower: Queen Anne's lace

Rr river, rocks, roots, ringtailed raccoons, rainbow trout, reptile

Ss spruce, spider web, spider, skunk, shoreline, saplings, stump, salmon, shadows, squirrel, snake, stones, soil, slope, stream

Tt tracks, trees, train, town, timberline, tunnel, tourists; bird: Western Tanager

Uu u-turn sign, u-shaped valley (scoured out by a retreating glacier), ungulate (any animal with hoofs like horse, deer or this elk), University College of the Cariboo sticker, sign to Unicorn Peak

Vv valley, vertical slope, vegetation, victim

Ww wooden window, water, winter, walking, Waterton Lakes National Park map, wolf, wapiti (another name for elk), watch, walrus carving; bird: woodpecker; flowers: wax plant

Xx x-country skiers, wildlife x-ing sign

Yy a "Y" in the road, yearlings, yellowjacket; flowers: yellow goldenrod, yarrow

Zz zigzag path, flowers: zigadenus or Death Camas (a very poisonous plant)

A Autumn is awesome in the mountains! When the aspen leaves turn yellow, it is as if bright lights were shining when you drive under the canopy of trees. Golden, a small town at the edge of the Rocky Mountains in British Columbia, is truly golden in the fall. In spring, avalanches often tumble down the slopes taking along much vegetation.

B A boreal forest is a northern forest made up mostly of coniferous (needle) trees often mixed with a few deciduous (leafy) trees. The black bear is munching on buffalo berries (Shepherdia canadensis). He will stock up on body fat before going into hibernation, sometime after the first snowfall. The bighorn is upwind and has obviously not noticed the bear yet. Whoever left the pack there was wise to retreat. Black bears are unpredictable but if you make enough noise while hiking, chances are you'll never surprise one.

C Rock-climbing is a popular sport in the mountains. Equipped with harnesses, ropes and helmets, climbers learn how to use their hands and feet to find support on the rock face. When they reach the top, they rappel or free-fall down. Climbers usually work in teams, and while reaching the top of a mountain is an exhilarating experience, safety is their first concern. Other mountain sports include cross-country and downhill skiing, hiking and mountain biking.

D Hiking quietly in the woods, in spring or early summer, you can come across a scene like this. Observing wildlife in their natural surroundings is an exciting experience. The mountains seem to hold their breath as you watch a grizzly from a safe distance, see a deer in a clearing, or observe a spider making its delicate web. And you realize that all lives are intricately connected.

E The cool fall evening mist rising off the lake sets the tone for one of the most mysterious sounds I have ever heard: the bugling of elk. This haunting, trumpet-like sound echoes through the mountains during "the rut" or mating season. The bugling is followed by the clashing of antlers as males fight over females. The ermine on the log is soon going to change to its white winter coat.

F Clear, cold mountain streams are a fisherman's paradise. Equipped with a fly rod and hipwaders, this fisherman will likely catch his quota of trout in no time. He has already caught four and the fox smells them! All summer, fireweed lights up the roadsides. It is appropriately named because it is one of the first flowers to flourish again after a forest fire.

G High in the alpine meadows lives the grizzly bear. This one is digging for a favorite snack: the larvae of insects. He also loves groundhogs, but the groundhog is laughing behind the bear's back because he can escape by using his many underground tunnels. The grizzly is larger than the black bear and easily recognized by the large hump on its back.

H When you go for a hike in the mountains, bring a good map. Even when hiking an established trail, it is easy to get lost. In many parks, including Banff National Park, mountain sheep may seem tame but, as with all wildlife, it is important to respect their natural state and not feed them. Helicopters are used for sightseeing and for mountain rescues. They transport bear traps to move captured bears from populated areas to remote wilderness and can also carry tanks underneath to spray water on forest fires.

I Slowly the ski lift pulls you up to the top of a mountain. You step off and try not to slither backwards on your skis. Then you turn around and gasp at the beautiful view of snowy slopes, inviting moguls, and a valley shrouded in clouds below. You put on your goggles, tug your poles under your arms and . . . zoom down the slopes! Skiing, downhill or cross-country, and snowboarding are wonderful winter sports to enjoy in the mountains.

J Jogging in the mountains can be surprisingly difficult if you are not used to the altitude! Breathing is harder and you run out of energy much faster than at a lower elevation. World class athletes often train at high-altitude training centers to build up their stamina.

K Mountain water is so clear that from your kayak, you can see rocks and minerals glittering on the bottom. It is also so clear that it may be safe to drink but it is wise to boil it first. Brilliant red Kokanee salmon struggle up the creek to their spawning grounds while a kingfisher waits impatiently for a minnow to dart by.

L At first, the call of a loon echoing across a silent lake sounds spooky. But soon you come to love that special call of the wild. It's fun to watch loons as they dive under water and to guess where they will surface again. They can stay submerged for five minutes or more! These particular loons enjoy a stop-over on glacier-fed Lake Louise in Alberta. Tourists from all around the world come here and it is a favorite honeymoon destination. It is very common for the weather to change rapidly in the mountains. One minute it can be sunny, the next minute the sky can burst into a fury of lightning. Many people in the mountains will tell you "if you don't like the weather, wait five minutes!"

M Early morning when the mountains first wake up is often the best time to be out for a walk. Stand still, listen to the silence while a bird lands just in front of you or a deer quietly approaches the water's edge. Once the sun burns the mist off the lake and the world has awakened, things aren't quite so magical.

N The silence of night, broken only by the crackling of flames, the hoot of an owl, and the singing of songs around the campfire. A warm sweater to ward off the coolness sunset brings. The smell of hotdogs and marshmallows roasting over the hot ashes. All these, combined with the stories of the park's interpreter about the invisible creatures beyond the light of the fire, make for wonderful memories of summer nights spent in the mountains.

O One summer, I was quietly sitting on a rock, enjoying the view, when an otter's head popped up from the water just in front of me. It's always a thrill to observe an animal in its natural surroundings, but I had never before seen the playful otter. I sat very still and watched him glide through the water. Then, with a flick of his sleek tail he disappeared quietly into the dark depths where otters can swim for well over two minutes before having to surface to breathe again.

P During the busy summer months when many tourists visit the mountains, parking areas can be very crowded. Campers, motorhomes, overheating cars, and van loads full of kids and dogs gather here to stretch, relax and take photos of the scenery. Picnic areas offer out-houses, bear-proof garbage cans, and also space to run. Once you shake the sillies out, it's time to get in the car again and drive over the next summit to your holiday destination.

Q Porcupines are unusual rodents. Each one carries approximately 30,000 barbed quills, which it uses to scare off predators! The porcupine feeds on bark, twigs and buds. The quartz, which glitters quietly in the sand, has helped to build up this shore.

R Ringtailed raccoons get much of their food from the water. These omnivores are adept at catching fish and eat almost anything else that is edible! At campsites, the masked bandits can be a real nuisance when they get into garbage cans or food supplies.

S One of earth's most intriguing mysteries is that of spawning salmon. Born in lakes and shallow streams, they swim out to sea. Years later, having traveled thousands of kilometers through the ocean, their remarkable instinct takes them back along rivers, battling currents, even leaping up waterfalls, to the very spot where they were born. Having turned a brilliant red, they die shortly after having laid and fertilized their eggs to ensure a new generation.

T Trains often travel through seemingly inaccessible valleys, across narrow bridges and through tunnels blasted out of solid rock. Tunnels protect the tracks from being wiped out by avalanches or rockslides.

U Trudging up mountains in sleek snow can be quite treacherous. Narrow hairpin roads don't allow for any turning around but pull-offs do let you pass a slower car. This car is on the way up to a ski area, but not to ski – on the roof of the car is a snowboard! Another way to get around in winter is by snowmobile.

V The difference between safety and danger can be one wrong step in the mountains. The terrain, the weather, everything can change suddenly. It's wise to be well prepared when going on an outing. Members of mountain rescue teams often put their own lives in danger to help someone in trouble. Here, a helicopter and a park ranger rescue a victim off a rock ledge by slinging him down.

W When heavy snow blankets the world and muffles all sounds, life seems to have come to a halt. But when you look and listen closely, you'll notice lots of activity going on. Mice scurry below the snow, tracks criss-cross in all directions, birds are busy foraging. All animals adapt to winter, some by going south, some by hibernating.

X Crossing the highway is dangerous to animals. Some mountain areas have special wildlife crossing signs to warn motorists to drive with care. Sometimes there are tunnels under the highway for animals to use.

Y These moose yearlings have a face only a mother could love! But even if moose aren't pretty, they are well suited for their environment. Their long legs allow them to wade through swamps where they consume many kilograms of plants, twigs and bark. Though usually calm, a male moose in rutting season is an extremely dangerous animal.

Z Even though mountain goats can weigh well over a hundred kilograms, they clamber up narrow ledges and icy slopes without stumbling. Their hoofs are actually skidproof. They spend much time above the timberline, searching for lichens and grasses. Both males and females have black, dagger-like horns. Little mountain goats are called kids!

Dedication of the Author

To Arnout, born in Banff: Climb every mountain,
follow every dream. . . .

Margriet Ruurs

Dedication of the Artist

To the innocence of children, the beauty of nature, and
the love of my family Lynn, Rita and Lee.

Andrew Kiss

The author and illustrator would like to express their sincere thanks to Ron Chamney of Interpretive and Educational Services, Kananaskis Country, for his generous help, support and input. Special thanks also to Arjun Basu for believing in us.

First published in hardcover in 1996
00 99 98 97 96 5 4 3 2 1

First published in paperback in 1996
00 99 98 97 96 5 4 3 2 1

Published in Canada by Tundra Books, Toronto, Ontario M5G 2E9

Published in the United States by Tundra Books of Northern New York, Plattsburgh, N.Y. 12901

Library of Congress Catalog Number: 96-60349

Canadian Cataloguing in Publication Data:

Ruurs, Margriet, 1952 -
    A mountain alphabet

ISBN 0-88776-374-X

    1. English language — Alphabet — Juvenile literature. 2. Rocky Mountains, Canadian (B.C. and Alta.) — Pictorial works — Juvenile literature.* I. Kiss, Andrew. II. Title.

PE1155.R88   1996   j421'.1   C96-900252-1

1st pbk. ed.
ISBN 0-88776-384-7

PE1155.R88   1996   j421'.1   C96-931266-0

The publisher has applied funds from its Canada Council block grant for 1996 toward the editing and production of this book.

Transparencies by Jim Shipley, Sector 49 Photography, Calgary

Printed in Hong Kong by South China Printing Co. Ltd.